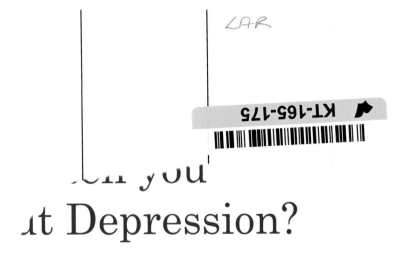

...ll you
it Depression?

Can I tell you about...?

The "Can I tell you about...?" series offers simple introductions to a range of limiting conditions and other issues that affect our lives. Friendly characters invite readers to learn about their experiences, the challenges they face, and how they would like to be helped and supported. These books serve as excellent starting points for family and classroom discussions.

Other subjects covered in the "Can I tell you about...?" series

ADHD

Adoption

Anxiety

Asperger Syndrome

Asthma

Autism

Cerebral Palsy

Dementia

Diabetes (Type 1)

Dyslexia

Dyspraxia

Eating Disorders

Eczema

Epilepsy

ME/Chronic Fatigue Syndrome

OCD

Parkinson's Disease

Pathological Demand Avoidance Syndrome

Selective Mutism

Stammering/Stuttering

Stroke

Tourette Syndrome

Can I tell you about Depression?

A guide for friends, family and professionals

CHRISTOPHER DOWRICK
AND SUSAN MARTIN
Illustrated by Mike Medaglia

Jessica Kingsley *Publishers*
London and Philadelphia

First published in 2015
by Jessica Kingsley Publishers
73 Collier Street
London N1 9BE, UK
and
400 Market Street, Suite 400
Philadelphia, PA 19106, USA

www.jkp.com

Copyright © Christopher Dowrick and Susan Martin 2015
Illustrations copyright © Mike Medaglia 2015

Library of Congress Cataloging in Publication Data
A CIP catalog record for this book is available from the Library of Congress

British Library Cataloguing in Publication Data
A CIP catalogue record for this book is available from the British Library

ISBN 978 1 84905 563 5
eISBN 978 1 78450 003 0

Printed and bound in Great Britain
by Bell and Bain Ltd, Glasgow

Contents

"So what is depression? It's a bit like being sad and tired. I'll tell you about that later, so that you can understand better if it happens to someone in your family, and not worry too much.

First, I'd like to tell you a bit about me and my family.

I'm 38 years old. I teach history in a secondary school. I'm usually well apart from my depression, but sometimes I get bouts of irritable bowel syndrome (sometimes called IBS), which causes pain in my tummy and makes me go to the toilet all the time. I know, euuch!

Jim's my husband. We met at college. We've been married for 15 years now. He's an accountant with a big company in the city. He is very good with numbers, and looks after all our bills. He's kind and friendly, though he doesn't really know how to talk about things like how he feels."

"We live in a comfortable house,
though we have a biggish mortgage
to pay off. I enjoy pottering around
in the back garden of an evening,
planting new flowers and weeding."

"We love going on holidays to hot places, especially Spain. We're trying to save up to buy an apartment there as we all like it so much.

We have two wonderful children, Helen and Andy. Helen is 13. She's very bright. She can speak Spanish better than Jim or me. She's a bit of a moody teenager these days, and has a great line in put-downs (especially to me). Andy is 11. Maths is his best subject in school. He is mad keen on football. He plays with his mates in the park. He's a regular on his junior school team ('attacking midfielder' he tells me, whatever that means). And he goes to all Liverpool's home games with his dad.

I think the world of them all, especially the kids. Usually I feel fine, but sometimes everything gets a bit too much for me.

Every few years I become depressed for a couple of months. I'm going to tell you what that's like, and how best to handle it."

"When I'm depressed the main thing
I'm aware of is how horrible I feel."

"I feel totally fed up, unhappy and miserable. Everything seems dark and grey. All colour has drained out of the world.

Sometimes it seems like I'm stuck inside a big thick bubble. I can see through the bubble all right to see what's happening – but everything and everyone outside seems distant and remote. I feel cut off.

Sometimes I feel scared and frightened as well, because I can't understand or control what's happening to me. At other times I don't even feel sad; I feel nothing at all. It's as if I'm empty inside; there is nothing in there.

I can't be bothered with anything when I'm depressed. I don't enjoy life. Nothing is interesting, not even my beautiful children or the flowers in my garden. The days are endless and very, very boring. I get things done when I have to but there's no fun in doing them, no pleasure.

This all makes me so tired. I feel tired, all the time. It doesn't matter how much sleep I've had, I have no energy. I'm exhausted. It's an effort to do anything. I feel so heavy, like gravity has increased or there's an enormous weight on my shoulders, pushing me down. Sometimes it's all I can do to get out of bed and get dressed, and I feel completely worn out when I've done that."

"When I look at myself in the bathroom mirror all I can see is an old, wrinkly woman who's wearing messy clothes and needs a good wash and a hair-do."

"Lots and lots of dark thoughts rattle around inside my head and it's very hard to stop them. Mostly I think about how useless I am, how I'm a failure and a complete waste of space. When I look at myself in the bathroom mirror all I can see is an old, wrinkly woman who's wearing messy clothes and needs a good wash and a hair-do.

I feel guilty about everything. I tell myself I should pull myself together and get back to teaching history in school. I blame myself for not being a good enough mother and for letting Helen and Andy down. I either ignore them completely or else shout at them if they're late getting up for school or watching TV when they should be doing their homework. I worry I'm not giving them the love they need to grow up into happy and healthy adults.

I think life is hopeless but there's no point in trying to do anything about it. If I do try to make things better I am bound to fail, and then I'll just be in an even worse mess than I already am. Sometimes I wonder if it'd be better for my family if I wasn't around anymore. I know they'd be a bit upset for a while, but wouldn't they forget about me soon enough? Then maybe they could get on with a better, happier life. But then I think I'd miss them all too much, so I'm just stuck here."

"Well, you've probably realised by now that I don't do very much when I'm depressed. I spend a lot of time just sitting on my sofa."

"I stay in bed, or else sit on my sofa in the living room. I can't be bothered to wash or get dressed properly. Every little thing is such an effort. I often wake up very early in the morning and can't get back to sleep again. I wish I could though, because time passes more quickly when you're asleep. Generally I feel worse in the morning, and maybe just a bit less awful as the day goes on.

I can't be bothered to do things with Helen and Andy. They might see it as a good thing that I don't nag them so much about having a bath or cleaning their teeth! But I get irritated with them when they ask me things or even want to tell me things. It's not that I'm not interested: I'm just too tired to think about anyone else.

I can't go into school. The idea of teaching history to all those young people is too overwhelming to even think about.

I watch a lot of TV – all the daytime shows and the soaps – but it's really just to pass the time; I'm not really interested in what's going on. I might try to pick up a book or a magazine but I can't concentrate properly and usually find I'm stuck on the first page, not taking any of the words in or even making much sense of the photos."

"Fortunately Jim doesn't mind
doing the weekly shop."

"If I get as far as the garden, I might think I want to do some weeding (the garden is getting very overgrown) but then I find I just can't be bothered, or else I spend ages and ages weeding one tiny bit of one flowerbed and then give up.

Cooking has gone out of the window. I just can't summon up the energy to make anything. The best I can manage is to heat up some ready meals in the microwave. I'm not interested in eating much. I'll just pick at a few bits if I have to. Fortunately Jim doesn't mind doing the weekly shop. He will sometimes make the kids their evening meal, or else bring in a take-away. They are both old enough to make their own school lunches, thank goodness, and Helen makes sure Andy doesn't just put junk in his lunch box.

When I'm depressed like this I can't see the point of having a day out with the family, like going to the cinema or out for a meal. And the thought of going on holiday in Spain, which I usually love, is much too much like hard work.

One of the worst things is that there seems no end to it. When I'm depressed it's as if I've always felt like this, and always will. I just can't remember that most of the time I feel fine."

"I first became depressed at college."

"The main thing I remember about growing up is that my father always thought I should work harder and do better. So I tried and tried to do well at everything – school work and sports and so on – but it was never enough. My mother was kinder but didn't seem to be able to stand up to Dad. That gave me the feeling that I had to be hard working and successful, or else people wouldn't like me.

The first time I remember becoming depressed was in college, where I was studying history. I was 19 and had just split up with a boyfriend who had been unkind. So I felt very miserable about that. It was about the time of our summer exams. I couldn't revise properly and failed one of the exams.

Breaking up with a boyfriend and then failing the exam confirmed in my head what a failure I was. I didn't want to live anymore. I bought lots of tablets from the chemist and was planning to take them all, so that I could go to sleep and never wake up. Fortunately my friend Anne knocked on my door that evening and found me before anything terrible happened."

"Anne persuaded me to go to
see the college doctor."

"The doctor was very understanding. She let me sit and cry in her office without making me feeling stupid. She prescribed me some antidepressant tablets and arranged for me to see a psychologist.

The psychologist was very helpful. I saw her six times over the summer holidays. We talked about lots of things, mainly my fear of being a failure. She helped me to see myself in a more positive light: as somebody who is worthwhile regardless of what I do or don't achieve in life.

We talked about my family as well. I realised my mother was also depressed sometimes. I'm not sure whether that means depression runs in our family, like a genetic thing, or whether it's because like me she found my father difficult to live with."

"I've been depressed five or six times since then. The next time was after Helen was born."

"It was wonderful to have her around, but my whole life was suddenly turned upside down. My hormones were all over the place, I wasn't getting any sleep, and Jim didn't know what to do. The doctor said it was 'baby blues' or post-natal depression and was quite common.

I was fine when Andy arrived, but then the next year Jim's business was in trouble and he was told he might lose his job. I started to worry about how we could possibly make ends meet with two small mouths to feed and I think that set me off again.

A couple of times it's seemed to come out of the blue, starting up for no reason I can think of. It links in with the stomach pains I get with my IBS, but I don't think that they are the cause of me getting depressed. They both just tend to happen at the same time.

I was very upset for quite a few months after my mother died five years ago. I'm not sure whether that was depression as such. Thinking about it now, it felt a bit different. Maybe that was the normal grief we all go through when we lose someone we love dearly."

"I've now worked out quite a few things that help me get better when I've been depressed."

"Some of them also make me less likely to get depressed again.

I tell Jim and the kids, and my good friends, that I may be quiet, miserable and bad-tempered for a while. I tell them it's not their fault or because of anything they've said or done to me. And I also tell them I know I'll get better because it's happened before. I just have to keep reminding myself at the moment.

When I'm feeling down and drained of energy I tell myself that it's OK to rest. It's a bit like hibernation: you know, the way animals such as tortoises and polar bears slow down and go to sleep for months to survive the cold, dark winters.

Instead of criticising myself all the time, I try to be kind to myself. I tell myself that I'm ill, and that this isn't something I'm doing on purpose. I remind myself of what I am good at, that I'm not a complete failure. For example, how I have brought two wonderful children into the world."

"Each day I see if I can do one thing I
enjoy, and one thing that I need to do.
They are often very small and simple
things, like smelling the scent of the flowers
in the garden or washing my hair."

"If I have a little more energy I sometimes go for a brief spin on my bike, or else help out for an hour or so in our local charity shop. I feel a bit better when I've done things like that.

I visit my family doctor every few weeks. Just talking to him helps, as he is very understanding. We always discuss what might help me get through a bad patch. If I'm really down I take antidepressant tablets for a few months. They do seem to speed up my recovery, though I have to be careful they don't make my IBS worse. I had more therapy sessions with a psychologist and after my mum died I saw the practice counsellor for a while.

Since I was last depressed two years ago, I have started something called 'mindfulness meditation'. This is a group where we learn how to relax our minds and just accept how we feel, without being cross with ourselves or trying to sort things out. It sounds a bit weird but it works. I love it!"

"A lot of kids worry that it must be their fault
if one of their parents gets ill or unhappy."

"But it isn't. I remember when Helen was five or six, she said to me, 'Sorry I've been naughty, Mummy, I'll try to be good. I promise you I'll behave better in future so you don't get sad again.' That's all wrong. It's not Helen's fault I get depressed, or Andy's for that matter. It often isn't anybody's fault. As I've explained to you, sometimes it just happens.

It's not Helen and Andy's job to look after me or make me better. That's for me and other grown-ups to sort out. The three jobs for children are to be respectful to others, responsible for yourself – and, most important, enjoy life as much as possible.

If your mum (or your dad) gets depressed, try not to worry too much. Don't blame yourself. It's not your fault. Allow them time and space to work through their problems. Give them a little hug from time to time and tell them you love them. Ask another grown-up to help them; don't try to do it yourself."

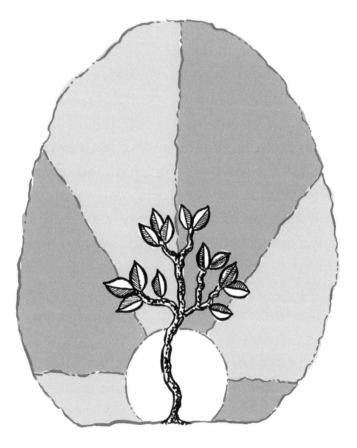

"It's important to enjoy life
as much as possible."

"Don't assume because your mum or dad gets depressed then you will, too. It doesn't usually work like that.

If you are loved and looked after, most likely you will grow up without any big worries to carry round.

Do carry on having fun. I tell Helen and Andy that is so important for me that they do have fun. It helps me to know they're still having a good life, even if I'm not feeling so good.

And remember, things will get better."

"Jim's learnt that it helps if he gives me a hug and tells me that he loves me, that he knows things will get better for me because they always have before."

"Jim's not very good at knowing how people feel, bless him, but he is solid as a rock. And that's exactly what I need when I'm feeling down. He's always the same; he's dependable. He doesn't seem to get stressed or angry when I ignore him or have a go at him.

Jim's learnt that it helps if he gives me a hug and tells me that he loves me, that he knows things will get better for me because they always have before. He looks after practical things like the shopping and washing, and even does a bit of hoovering from time to time so I don't have to worry the house is descending into chaos. And he's great at making sure Helen and Andy have enough to eat, get to school on time and do their homework. Sometimes if I'm going through a really bad patch he'll take time off work to look after me.

I'm not sure what I'd do without him to be honest."

"I've got some good friends, too."

"There's a couple from college who I still see, and three of the other teachers from my school. They take it in turns to call in to see me in the afternoon or early in the evening. Sometimes they do the shopping so Jim doesn't have to. They don't seem to mind if I just sit there and cry, or tell them how awful I'm feeling. I worry that I'll make them depressed, too – that my illness must be catching. But they assure me it's OK, they are fine, they are there for me. If I have a bit of energy they'll play Monopoly (my favourite board game) with me. I like it when Helen and Andy join in as well. For a few minutes at least I can lose myself in the game and forget about my worries.

Jim also remembers to arrange appointments for me to see my doctor and makes sure I get to my therapy sessions and the mindfulness group.

As you know, I find my family doctor very helpful, especially when I'm depressed.

So it's a mixture of all these things – what I can do for myself, the support of my family and friends, and help from doctors and therapists – that helps me to get better when I am depressed."

What is depression?

This chapter is intended mainly as a background guide for teachers and group leaders.

Depression is common. Between one in five and one in ten of us will experience an episode at least once during our lifetime. It can be a one-off event, but for many people it does recur from time to time. For some people depression is a persistent, long-term problem.

Depression is more common among women than men, and is more likely to occur during early middle age. We decided to focus on Julie's story in this book because it is fairly typical. She is a woman in her 30s with a history of recurrent depressive episodes.

DIAGNOSING DEPRESSION

The two main things that are needed to make a diagnosis of depression are *low mood* and *loss of interest or pleasure* in normal activities. These should be present most of the time for at least two weeks. In addition, the diagnosis needs at least three of the following to be present most of the time:

- significant weight gain or weight loss (without dieting)

- sleeping too much or too little

- being either restless or slowed down, as noted by others

- fatigue or loss of energy

- feeling worthless or inappropriately guilty

- reduced ability to think or concentrate, or make decisions

- recurrent thoughts of suicide, meaning deliberately causing one's own death.

You will see that Julie describes most of these symptoms when she is telling us about her experiences of being depressed.

Before making a diagnosis of depression, doctors need to take four additional things into account:

1. At least one of the current symptoms must be either depressed mood, or else loss of interest or pleasure in activities. Julie has both of these symptoms when she is depressed.

2. The symptoms should cause significant impairment of social, occupational or other important areas of functioning. That is to say, they should interfere with the person's ability to lead their usual daily life. This is certainly the case for Julie when she is depressed.

3. The symptoms should not be due to the direct effects of medication or a drug of abuse (such as cannabis or heroin); or due to a general medical condition, for example, hypothyroidism. Julie's symptoms are not due to drugs or alcohol. Her medical condition, IBS, is not a direct cause of her depression.

4. And, finally, the symptoms should not be better accounted for by bereavement after the loss of a loved one. This last point is very important, as grief reactions are common to all of us and are not the same as depressive episodes. Julie notices this herself when she describes how her feelings after her mother died seemed different from her other episodes of depression.

We must be careful not to over-diagnose depression. Many people who experience intense sadness after traumatic events, such as an accident or an assault, the break-up of a relationship or losing a job, are probably reacting normally to the stress of the situation rather than experiencing depression.

CAUSES OF DEPRESSION
The causes of depression are often divided into two types: predisposing and precipitating.

Predisposing or vulnerability factors are things in our backgrounds that make us more likely to become depressed.

Depression can run in families. Julie notices that, like her, her mother became depressed from time to time. This may be because there is an in-built, genetic programme that makes some people more likely to become depressed. It may also be because some family set-ups are more depressing than others. In Julie's case it is difficult to be sure which of these is more likely. There could be a genetic element, in that she and her mother both get depressed. But there is also the problem of her father, who is severe and sets very high standards for her and her mother.

Certain personality types, particularly people who tend to worry a lot, are more likely to become depressed. So are people who have had difficult times in childhood. These difficulties may be caused by a highly critical parent, as in Julie's case. They may sometimes be worse than that, for example if a child has been neglected or has been the victim of physical or sexual abuse.

Precipitating or trigger factors are things that happen in our lives today that can spark off an episode of depression. These can be events in our lives that we find difficult to cope with, such as an illness, or a problem in work or within the family. Julie's first episode of depression was triggered by losing her boyfriend and failing her exams. One of her later episodes of depression was sparked off by her worries about Jim losing his job.

It probably needs both predisposing and precipitating factors to set off an episode of depression.

EFFECTS OF DEPRESSION

As we can see from Julie's story, depression has a huge impact on the person who is suffering from it and on their loved ones.

It also has a big effect on society as a whole. Many people have to take time off work, either because they are themselves depressed or in order to take care of someone with depression. This is the case for Julie, and sometimes for Jim, too.

By the year 2030, depression is likely to cause more disability and death worldwide than any other health problem except HIV/AIDS. In high-income countries, such as Canada, England and the USA, depression will have more effect on disability and mortality than every other health problem, more even than heart disease or dementia.[1]

TREATING DEPRESSION

We can do a lot to help ourselves when we are depressed, and also to reduce the chances of becoming depressed. The New Economics Foundation (NEF) has identified five ways to wellbeing:

- *Connect:* keep in touch with the people around you

- *Be Active:* exercise makes you feel good

- *Take Notice:* be aware of the world around you and how you are feeling

- *Keep Learning:* try something new

- *Give:* do something nice for someone else.
  (adapted from NEF Five Ways to Wellbeing)

These are simple actions that we can all take, and that help to improve our wellbeing. You will notice that Julie manages to do some of these things, such as being active on her bicycle, taking notice of the flowers in her garden and giving time to charity work.

There are two main ways in which family and friends can help someone who is depressed:

- The first is simply being there for the person, not giving up on them or getting fed up with them: offering them warmth and kindness and keeping a

---

1   Mathers, C., Boerma, T. and Ma Fat D. (2008) *The Global Burden of Disease – 2004 Update.* Geneva: World Health Organisation.

positive, hopeful attitude that they will get better in time.

- The second is providing them with practical day-to-day help with things that they are not able to do for themselves when they are depressed.

You will see that Jim, even though he isn't much good at expressing feelings, is very helpful to Julie in both of these ways. He doesn't get stressed or flustered by her depression, and he does do lots of extra housework and other practical tasks.

There are two main categories of psychosocial help that are effective for people with depression:

- *Low-intensity interventions:* these include computerised self-help materials, physical activity programmes and group reading programmes. They are most helpful for people with mild to moderate depression. People can often access these directly for themselves.

- *High-intensity interventions:* these include cognitive-behavioural therapy (CBT), behavioural activation, problem-solving treatment and counselling for depression. They are most helpful for people with moderate to severe depression. People may need to be referred for these interventions by their doctor.

Antidepressant drug treatments do not make much difference to people with mild depression. They are most likely to be helpful for people with severe depression. They can be prescribed by family doctors, who can advise on how to take them and on possible side effects. It is usually recommended to take a course of antidepressant drugs for about six months.

For people like Julie, who suffer from recurrent depression, taking antidepressant drugs long term may reduce the risk of further episodes. There is also good evidence that mindfulness training – that Julie tells us about – is protective against further bouts of depression.

Most people with depression can manage it themselves and with the help of their family doctor. However, some people may need to see a specialist, usually a psychiatrist. This might be if they are not responding to treatment or are at high risk of suicide.

Recommended reading, websites and organisations

BOOKS FOR CHILDREN AND TEENS
Fiction which includes child perspectives on adult depression

Hornby, N. (1998) *About a Boy*. London: Penguin.

There is also a 2002 film of the same name, directed by the Weitz brothers. Twelve-year-old Marcus and his depressed mother Fiona are central characters.

BOOKS FOR FRIENDS, FAMILY AND PROFESSIONALS
Background reading on depression that emphasises non-medical approaches

Dowrick, C. (2009) *Beyond Depression* (second edition). Oxford: Oxford University Press.

Dowrick, C. and Frances, A. (2013) "Medicalising unhappiness." *British Medical Journal 347*:f7140.

WEBSITES
Headspace
Headspace provide an excellent introduction to meditation and mindfulness.
www.getsomeheadspace.com

Healthtalkonline

Healthtalkonline provides first-hand accounts of people's experiences of depression. These are available in both video and text form.
www.healthtalkonline.org/peoples-experiences/mental-health/depression/topics

New Economics Foundation (NEF)

You can find more details about the New Economics Foundation's "Five Ways to Wellbeing" at:
www.neweconomics.org/projects/entry/five-ways-to-well-being

Royal College of Psychiatrists (RCP)

The Royal College of Psychiatrists provides information about depression.
www.rcpsych.ac.uk/healthadvice/problemsdisorders/depression.aspx

Wellbecoming

And we write our own good mental health blog, called Wellbecoming. You can find it on:
www.wellbecoming.blogspot.com

ORGANISATIONS
UK

Depression Alliance
20 Great Dover Street
London
SE1 4LX
Voicemail: 0845 123 23 20
Email: information@depressionalliance.org
Website: www.depressionalliance.org

Depression Alliance is a charity based in England that provides information and support services for people with depression.

MIND

15–19 Broadway
Stratford
London
E15 4BQ
Phone: 020 8519 2122
Fax: 020 8522 1725
Email: contact@mind.org.uk
Website: www.mind.org.uk

MIND is a mental health charity based in England that advocates for people with depression and other mental health problems.

USA

National Alliance on Mental Illness (NAMI)

3803 N. Fairfax Dr., Ste. 100
Arlington, VA 22203
Phone: (703) 524 7600
Fax: (703) 524 9094
Website: www.nami.org

NAMI is a grassroots mental health organisation dedicated to building better lives for the millions of Americans affected by mental illness.

CANADA

Canadian Mental Health Association

1110–151 Slater Street
Ottawa, ON K1P 5H3
Fax: 613 745 5522
Website: www.cmha.ca/about-cmha

Canadian Mental Health Association promotes the mental health of all and supports the resilience and recovery of people experiencing mental illness.

AUSTRALIA

Beyond Blue
PO Box 6100 Hawthorn West
Victoria
Australia 3122
Phone: 03 9810 6100
Fax: 03 9810 6111
Website: www.beyondblue.org.au

Beyond Blue is an independent, not-for-profit organisation working to increase awareness and understanding of anxiety and depression in Australia and to reduce the associated stigma.